MW00960512

Your Great Book Ot

Tax Liens and Deeds Investing

The Beginner's Real Estate Guide To Earning Sustainable Passive Income

Phil C. Senior

Bluesource And Friends

This book is brought to you by Bluesource And Friends, a happy book publishing company.

Our motto is **"Happiness Within Pages"**

We promise to deliver amazing value to readers with our books.

We also appreciate honest book reviews from our readers.

Connect with us on our Facebook page www.facebook.com/bluesourceandfriends and stay tuned to our latest book promotions and free giveaways.

Tax Liens And Deeds Investing

Tax Liens And Deeds Investing

By reading this document, the reader agrees that under no circumstances is the author responsible for any losses, direct or indirect, that are incurred as a result of the use of the information contained within this document, including, but not limited to, errors, omissions, or inaccuracies.

Table of Contents

Tax Liens And Deeds Investing

Tax Liens And Deeds Investing

Conclusion

References

Introduction

If you've picked up this book, chances are that you've heard someone mentioning something about tax liens or deeds at a real estate seminar. Tax liens and deeds are mythical figures of real estate investment. Everyone's heard a little bit about them here and there, but when it comes to actual experience with them, more people seem to have sighted Bigfoot.

This book is going to introduce you to the profitable world of tax lien investing. One of the things that makes this topic difficult to understand is that there are a variety of rules and regulations in the United States surrounding this form of investment. Each state has its own way of doing things and the dynamics of how sales work also differ from one county to the next.

Then there are the laws. Every real estate investor needs to be up to speed on the laws surrounding their investment, but they take a special meaning when it comes to tax liens and deeds. You need to conduct your research thoroughly, and for the beginner investor, it will seem as if there are a million things to take care of.

Tax Liens And Deeds Investing

Well, this is where this book is going to help you. If you've ever wondered how you could earn a steady rate of return on your money without undertaking huge financial risks, then tax lien investing is the right choice for you. Tax deeds are slightly different instruments, and they do require a higher financial outlay.

However, they offer the savvy investor an opportunity to buy properties at rates far lower than what they're worth. If you're the kind of investor who loves buying foreclosures and REOs (Real Estate Owned - typically by a bank or a government entity), then tax deeds will be a natural fit for you. Best of all, you could stand to make even more.

The first question that people ask is, if tax lien and deeds investing is so profitable, how is it that no one seems to have heard about it? Quite simply: Competition. Tax liens and deeds are sold by states through auctions. The more investors there are present at these auctions, the greater is the chance that everyone is going to have to settle for a less lucrative deal.

After all, everyone's going to bid the prices down. The second reason is that the big boys themselves are in on the action and there isn't much room for a broker or a middleman to make money. Think about all the advertisements you've encountered over the years in the industry. Chances are, all of them were offering you a middleman service, or something connected to you having to part with your cash.

There's no such room in this investment arena. As a result, tax lien investing hides in plain sight.

Why Liens?

So why should you invest in these forms of real estate? After all they're just pieces of paper. For starters, how does securing the right to the property before a mortgage sound? This is just one of the many advantages that liens and deeds offer their investors. A lien on a property is senior to all forms of debt - including mortgages. The only exception is if the county places a health-related lien on the property.

However, as an investor who holds the tax lien (or deed) on the property, you're the senior creditor. This is why banks themselves invest in tax liens prolifically. Some of the biggest investors in these instruments happen to be institutions.

Tax Liens And Deeds Investing

Whenever the stock market crashes, the tax lien market witnesses a huge rush, which results in increased competition at auctions. This is because savvy institutions know where the money is when times in the stock market get rough. High net worth individuals also invest in lien and deeds through specially-structured funds.

This doesn't mean you cannot partake in these instruments. If anything, you have an advantage over the big players because you can purchase smaller deals that offer huge returns on your investment. What's more, some of the best deals can be found in markets that institutions don't bother looking at for various reasons.

In this book, you're going to learn how tax liens work. You'll understand how the investment ought to be structured, and some of the pitfalls of investing in them. That's right! Despite the lucrative nature of these instruments, there is a danger of making a mistake and taking a loss.

Once you've learned about tax liens, you'll learn all about tax deeds. Deeds differ from liens in that they carry more obligations on your part. Besides, some states issue deeds thanks to the laws that are in operation. You're going to learn all about these laws and how you can approach your deals in an intelligent manner.

Why Tax Liens and Deeds?

Real estate investments are often contrasted with stock market investments because these are the two main drivers of wealth creation in America. It's only logical that we compare and contrast tax lien investing with stock market investing. Over the past 100 years, the stock market has returned 10% per year on average (Cussen, 2020).

There is no such data on tax lien investing since so much depends on the individual deal as well as the care with which the investor has approached a deal. However, a cursory glance at some of the returns that states offer in auctions is instructive. In Florida for example, investors can earn a safe 12-16% on their money.

These rates vary depending on the county and the state. However, such returns are not unheard of. Perhaps the only disadvantage that tax liens pose is that there's no easy way for the investor to compound their money automatically. With stocks, you can leave your investment as it is and you'll continue to earn money.

With tax liens and deeds, you'll have to sell and then reinvest your money. However, this disadvantage is countered by simply preparing in advance and knowing how to spot good deals. Besides, the higher rate of return compensates the investor for any time that funds might lie dormant.

The bottom line is that tax lien and deeds investing is an extremely lucrative field to explore. It's been around for a long time, but due to a combination of factors, it remains relatively untouched. This reduces the competition you'll face, and thus your chances of making a high rate of return increases.

Let's now move forward and take a look at what tax liens are and how they work.

Chapter 1: Tax Liens 101

So what is a tax lien and why should you be investing in them? The origin of a tax lien begins with, you guessed it, taxes. All property in the United States is taxed by the authorities to fund local services. In a municipality's case, this would be things like: The fire department, community centers, the sheriff's department, maintenance of parks, etc.

Local governments have multiple streams of revenue, but taxes are one of the primary streams. This stream is composed of income taxes as well as property taxes. While income taxes are collected at the state levels, property taxes go directly to the county where the property is physically located.

With taxes, comes delinquency. Often, property owners don't pay their taxes for one reason or another and this creates a problem for the local government. If people don't pay their taxes, how can they fund their services? How can they pay salaries to staff and run essential services that citizens require?

Investors

The best way to address this problem is to turn to investors who can help the county bridge the gap between their expenses and revenues. The county auctions these liens to investors and requires them to pay the outstanding property taxes. In exchange for this, the county pays the investor an interest rate.

The auction determines the interest rate being paid. In some states, this is referred to as a penalty. Typically, states fix the auction rate and bidding commences on a sliding scale. For example, Florida's rates begin at 18% and usually settle around 12-15% depending on what the stock market looks like.

It seems odd but auction rates depend on stock market performance. This is because when stocks get hammered, institutional investors look to place money in alternative investments, with tax liens being one of the most preferred. This increases competition at auctions since large sums of cash are thrown around by them and this depresses interest or penalty rates.

What you must understand is that these interest rates are fixed but are far from guaranteed. Once the auction is complete, the property owner will have a time limit within which they must pay the outstanding taxes. This period can range from a few months to four years.

Typically, the redemption period lasts for around two years. This is a good thing for investors since the longer the owner takes to pay their taxes, the greater is the amount of money you earn on your investment. If the investor does not pay the tax within the redemption period, you have the right to foreclose on the property.

Senior Lien

This is one of the biggest advantages of owning a tax lien. It is senior to all other forms of debt except prior tax liens and health-and-safety-related liens placed by the local government. For example, if the property was run down and if the local authorities had to clear weeds and disinfect the place, this money will need to be cleared prior to anything else.

However, tax liens are senior to mortgage debt and you have the option to foreclose on the property. I'll cover the foreclosure process and your options in a later chapter. For now, understand that your liens are secured by property.

In terms of payment, you don't need to worry about collecting or following up with the property owner. The owner makes their payment before the redemption period to the government, and once they're paid, the government cuts you a check for your investment amount plus interest. That's all there is to it.

The income that you earn from this investment is considered ordinary income, and you'll pay the marginal tax rate associated with your tax bracket.

States

Not every state in America issues tax liens. In fact, roughly half the states follow the tax lien model while the rest follow a tax deed or a hybrid model. You'll learn more about tax deeds later, but for now, understand that the purchase of a tax deed equals the purchase of a property.

Tax Liens And Deeds Investing

In that method, the local government recovers the property taxes due through the sale of the property itself. The hybrid method also involves the sale of property, but the original owner has the opportunity to pay their taxes upon which they receive the title to the property. The investor who purchased the deed gets paid interest (or penalties) according to the rate agreed upon previously.

Here is a list of states that allow tax lien investing:

- Alabama
- Arizona
- Colorado
- District of Columbia
- Florida
- Illinois
- Indiana
- Iowa
- Kentucky
- Maryland
- Mississippi
- Missouri
- Montana
- Nebraska
- New Jersey
- North Dakota
- Ohio

- Oklahoma
- South Carolina
- South Dakota
- Vermont
- West Virginia
- Wyoming

Ohio is technically a state that issues deeds. However, counties with populations greater than 200,000 issue liens.

The states below follow the hybrid model:

- Connecticut
- Delaware
- Georgia
- Hawaii
- Louisiana
- Massachusetts
- Pennsylvania
- Rhode Island
- Tennessee
- Texas

Pennsylvania is a deed state just like Ohio, but will issue liens if properties have been occupied for at least 90 days prior to the sale (Kelley, 2020).

Advantages

There are many advantages of tax lien investing. Here are a few of them.

Control

As an investor, you fully determine where you want to invest and in which property types. You can invest in residential properties, small commercial and even in large commercial properties. For example, many famous properties such as the Willis Tower (formerly the Sears Tower) in Chicago have been past due on their property taxes.

The liens are secured by the property itself, and this makes them a very safe form of investing. As I mentioned earlier, these liens are the senior-most debt connected to the property.

Secure

The entire process of issuing a lien, collecting payment and disbursing those payments to you is controlled by the government. This makes the possibility of fraud next to zero. Having said that, this doesn't mean you can't lose money. It's just that there are no Ponzi schemes or other marketing tactics being used to misdirect investors.

Time

The amount of time an investor needs to spend on this method is comparable to the average stock market investment. You'll need to get to know the property and the terms of the deal. You'll need to navigate the auction process in an efficient manner. You'll learn how to do this in a later chapter.

Investing in tax liens is far less time-consuming than other forms of real estate investment. The numbers involved are also a lot simpler to understand. You receive an interest rate and that's it. If the owner doesn't pay, you own the property. You don't need to memorize a bunch of rules of thumb or calculate ARVs.

Liquidity

This is an area of potential concern for investors. Your investment in the lien is an illiquid investment until the owner pays back their taxes. Sometimes, property owners might be able to pay their taxes immediately but will delay it for whatever reason. A common reason is because of them earning higher rates of return on their cash than the interest they need to pay.

Whatever the reason may be, this illiquidity of your investment isn't bad news. For starters, the longer the owner takes to pay, the more interest you earn. Secondly, your investment is secured by the property so it isn't as if you're sitting in dead cash. You're guaranteed to receive the funds (or property) at some point and this can lead to a potential windfall for you.

Legal Help

As an investor, you don't have to concern yourself with foreclosure processes or anything of the sort. The entire process is governed by the local authorities and as a result, you'll have the full weight of local law enforcement behind you. As such, this gives investors a wide safety net and reduces the already low possibility of encountering significant problems with your investment.

As you can see, these advantages make investing in tax liens a no-brainer. To summarize the process, here's how tax liens work:

1. Investor buys and receives a lien on the property. They do not receive a title to the property or any other rights.
2. They receive an interest rate (penalty from the existing owner's perspective) until the taxes are paid.
3. The existing owner has a period within which they must pay their taxes. This is called the "redemption period".
4. If this payment isn't made, the investor gains title to the property, assuming there are no prior property tax liens.

Here's how a hybrid system works:

1. Investor purchases the property and receives the title. However, the existing owner has the right to pay their taxes and get the property back.
2. If the owner pays their penalties and taxes within the redemption period, the investor receives interest plus principal back.
3. If not, the investor gains full control of the title.

Chapter 2: Types of Properties

A common misconception within the world of tax lien investing is that liens are available only on rundown or terribly-maintained properties. This is far from the truth. As I mentioned in the previous chapter, even the Willis Tower in Chicago had an outstanding tax lien on it.

Browse through old records and you'll notice that celebrities and other stars have had outstanding liens on their properties. What's more, many companies have had outstanding liens on their locations from time to time.

Property taxes are collected on all kinds of real estate, and this means you're liable to find all sorts of properties on offer. They can be for homes in rich neighborhoods to commercial property to large mixed-use buildings. You'll often find properties being listed that are owned by banks.

This happens because once banks foreclose on homes, they become liable for property taxes. Typically, banks wait to resell these properties to developers or other entities before paying the property taxes. This means tax lien investing isn't just about investing in rundown properties in poor neighborhoods.

Lien amounts run from $100 to over a million. It depends on the kind of property that is being offered.

Types of Investors

While the types of properties on offer are varied, there aren't too many different types of investors involved. Almost all investors are either individual real estate investors, or are institutions looking to earn returns on the money their investors have placed with them. These institutions could be hedge funds or other private equity funds.

Often, you'll notice private equity funds housed under large Wall Street banks bidding for liens at these auctions. I must note that there are different types of auctions that states conduct. Each state conducts only one type of auction and has a single set of policies associated with their repayment and investment.

You'll learn more about auctions in a later chapter and about investment returns in the next one. At this point, it's important to take note of how the competition thinks. As I mentioned earlier, low-interest-rate environments and sinking stock markets prompt institutions to flood the tax lien space (Kelley, 2020).

It isn't just liens but deeds that get flooded as well. For the most part, this isn't great news for the individual. A lot of states operate what is called a "bid-down" auction structure. For example, Florida starts its auctions at 18% and attendees bid this rate down.

Institutions in a low-interest rate environment such as the one we're in are likely to bid as low as 0.25%. This is a ridiculously low rate of return but it still works out thanks to the way the state structures the auctions. You'll learn more about this in the next chapter.

For now, keep in mind that institutions have deep pockets and purchase as many liens as possible to satisfy the needs of their investors. If you happen to spot many of these investors in the audience, your odds of winning an auction are low.

Typically, the best properties get bid down to single digits by investors, irrespective of whether they're institutions or individuals. This is easy enough to understand. A well-maintained and occupied property is less of a headache, and if the owner happens to default, the lien investor can then stand to own a great property for a fraction of the price.

Run-down properties that require a lot of work will typically sell close to the statutory or advertised rate. It's entirely possible to score great deals with a little bit of homework. Some states tend to offer better properties than others. Texas is a case in point.

Texas

Texas defines its properties as belonging to two categories: Homestead or Non-homestead. A homestead property is an agricultural one. These properties have a two-year redemption period and attract a penalty of 25% for the first year and 50% for the second year. Note that the word 'penalty' is different from 'interest'.

I've used the word 'penalty' as being equivalent to interest in the previous chapter, but that was when talking about payment from the standpoint of the owner. From an investor's perspective (and the county's perspective) penalties are different from interest. I'll explain this in more detail in the next chapter.

The auctions in Texas tend to offer high rates of return thanks to their penalty system, and properties tend to be better maintained on average. The reason for this isn't really known and, frankly, it doesn't matter.

I don't mean to say that Texas has the best returns on offer and therefore it's the only state you should invest in. Great deals can be found everywhere. You must pay special attention to how the laws surrounding the auction works and how the state will pay you the interest rate on your investment.

Some jurisdictions don't pay an interest rate but run a premium auction where you bid the final amount you want to receive at the end of the redemption period. All of these play a crucial role in determining your rate of return on your investment.

Reasons for Delinquency

A common question that investors ask is whether they should be worried about the reasons for delinquency on the property. The answer to this question depends on the goal you have in mind. If your aim is to own the property and hope for a default on the payment, then you probably don't care what the reason is. If you can purchase the property, then it's a win-win for you no matter what happens.

If your aim is to earn a steady interest rate on your investment, then you'll have to examine the reasons the owner is delinquent. In such cases, a fancy property is less likely to default than a rundown one. When it comes down to it though, you don't have to be all that worried about the specific reasons for default.

You will have to carry out research on the property as well as the type of neighborhood it's located in. Beyond this, you'll often find any number of reasons for default. One of the most common reasons is that the owner is outside the country or that the property is being managed by a firm that hasn't received a notice or invoice from the owner of the place and has thus defaulted on the payment.

Some investors niche themselves and buy only certain types of property. This choice is entirely up to you and depends on how comfortable you are with the process. Some investors prefer to own liens on residential real estate since their cash flow is more predictable than commercial units.

The prospect of owning the property is a real one, and you should take care when determining whether the type of property you're looking at is something you'd be comfortable owning. If not, it's safe to stay away from it.

Commercial real estate tends to move in a different cycle from residential real estate. It's tough to obtain financing for such properties and owning them involves issues that you won't encounter with residential real estate. For example, you'll need to take care of liability insurance in case someone gets injured while visiting your tenant.

This leads to competition for residential properties being higher than for commercial ones. This doesn't mean there aren't good deals to be had. It's just that you should do your homework and only stick to the ones that make sense for you to own. Sometimes, investors get carried away by the high rates of return on offer and end up owning properties that create headaches for them.

Chapter 3: Rates of Return

One of the great things about tax lien investing is that you can achieve an astronomical rate of return for very little work. Such instances are not typical, of course, but there's always a chance of earning it. For example, you might buy a lien and receive a check back with interest before you even pay the county.

Typically, the county charges auction participants a deposit and lumps this together with the cash that needs to be paid upon winning. The investor typically has a week or two to pay this amount in full. If the owner clears the lien within this time, you'll receive a check with an interest payment without having to put up a single cent of your own money above the deposit.

Understanding how to calculate your rate of return is important when it comes to tax liens. This can get a bit complicated because of how various states run their auctions. Let's look at the different kinds of payment structures states have in place and see if we can understand this better.

Fixed Interest

Some states such as Iowa offer a fixed interest payment on all of their liens. The state offers a fixed two-percent payment per month. In other words, your yearly interest rate is 24%. If the property owner redeems their payment within a year, you'll earn the interest payments for the number of months it took them to do so.

For example, if you purchased a lien and if the owner redeemed it after six months, you'll earn 12% interest on your investment. On an annualized basis, this is 24%. This is also the maximum return you will make on your investment since the state doesn't have any additional penalty fees.

This is a pretty simple scenario for an investor to figure out. Most beginner investors to tax liens would do well to stick to such liens since the return on investment calculation makes it easy for them to figure out how much money they can invest. This isn't to say that other states are complicated. It's just that the cash flow is predictable and you can project your returns easily.

Penalty

As I mentioned in the previous chapter, the term "penalty" is very different from interest rate as far as the investor in a lien and the government is concerned. Here's how a penalty works. The state, for example Texas, issues a statutory penalty rate (not interest rate.)

This rate is paid to the investor no matter how long the redemption period is. As you learned in the previous chapter, Texas has a penalty rate of 50% on the second year of the lien. Let's say the owner redeems their taxes after a month. You'll still receive 25% of your investment.

Contrast this to the previous section where the annual statutory rate is divided into 12 payments every month. Here, the penalty rate is imposed no matter when the owner pays. This means if you earn a 25% return within a month, you could earn an annual yield of 300% on your investment.

I must point out that 300% is not what you will actually earn. It assumes you earn 25% every month for a year which is a bit far-fetched. However, if you reinvest that sum into another lien and earn 25% for the rest of the year, you've just made 50%. If you leave the money lying as is and don't touch it for a year, you've still earned 25%.

If the owner doesn't pay their taxes well into the second year, you'll earn a payment of 50% on your investment. Assuming it took the owner 17 months to redeem their taxes, you'll earn a return or close to 2.9% per month. This works out to 35% per year. Pretty high, as you can see.

Another state that follows a penalty model is Georgia where the rate is 20%. I must point out that both of these states are hybrid states. This means you'll be bidding for the property title and not for the lien.

Minimum Interest

This policy is perhaps the most prevalent currently. Most states have what is called a "bid-down auction". This is where they'll declare a statutory rate and investors will then bid this rate down. The lowest bid wins. As I mentioned in the previous chapter, institutional investors might bid this down to as low as 0.25%.

Why does this make sense for them? Well, the answer lies in the minimum interest policy. Despite bidding just 0.25%, these states have minimum interest payments that they make. In the case of Florida, this works out to five percent. Thus, no matter how low the investor bids, the state will pay a minimum of five percent.

This changes the rate of return an investor can earn, and it now depends on how many months the owner takes to redeem their taxes. If they take two months to redeem, then the investor will have earned five percent in two months which equals a 30% annual return.

If the owner takes two years, then they'll have earned a return of 2.5% per year, which is pretty abysmal. However, there's another scenario that such states offer which makes a low bidding rate justifiable. If the owner defaults on their payment, the investor will have to file for the tax deed, which will give them ownership of the property.

Once the investor files for it, it takes the county around four to six months to arrange the sale of the property. In the interim, the investor is paid the statutory rate (not the rate that they bid) and this results in a massive boost in gains. Typically, statutory rates are around 18-20%, and earning this rate of interest pro-rated over a few months tends to give them satisfactory rates of return.

A common approach investors take is to purchase a basket of liens. This ensures that some lien will constantly be redeemed throughout the redemption period and this gives the investor a range of rates of return on their investment.

The "Best" States

At this point, a common question to ask is: Which is the best state to invest in? Given the variety of payout methods, it would seem as if the penalty system provides the best rate of return. On paper, this happens to be true.

In real life, it's an entirely different answer. The best state for you to invest in depends on your preferences. As a rule of thumb, it's best to invest in jurisdictions that are closest to you and have properties that you can easily view. You must also keep in mind that most counties will require you to be physically present at the auctions.

It sounds incongruous in this day and age, but a lot of counties and cities still conduct their auctions in person. There's no real reason for this other than bureaucratic stubbornness. Arizona leads the way in terms of migrating the majority of its auctions online.

However, the majority of counties are still offline, and this can add significant costs to your investment. If you happen to live in New York and are bidding on properties in Washington (the state), you're going to pay airfares that will be a significant portion of your investment amount. This doesn't include the cost of researching properties in person and staying there while this is carried out.

It's best to stick to what you know. If the county you're interested in is within driving distance, then you can reasonably bid on properties in it. If you can afford the costs and have a large roll of money to invest, then Texas and Georgia offer the best returns thanks to the penalty system.

States offering fixed interest payments are another good bet since it's simple to project how much you'll earn. Another great option is to invest in areas you'd like to vacation in and will travel to at least once a year. States such as Hawaii tend to attract competitive bids, but the large scale of investment in these states tend to create quite a few great opportunities.

Florida, especially the southern part of the state, tends to offer similar opportunities for investors. Take the time to study the official policies of the county and its payment process. You can do this by searching for tax lien auctions. Each county lists in detail the payment being offered as well as the auction process. You'll learn all about how the auctions work in the next chapter.

For now, understand that your rate of return will depend on a lot of things from the redemption period to the type of payment that's being offered. The penalty system offers the highest potential rate of return. If a high rate is all you're after, then this is your best bet.

However, don't chase returns just for their own sake. You should prioritize your peace of mind as well. The last place you want to find yourself is where you don't have a clue as to how the process works and you've just discovered that you've "won" something. Winning the auction is just the star, as you'll shortly learn.

Tax Liens And Deeds Investing

There are a number of dates and other conventions that come with the tax lien investing process. The next chapter is going to explain all of this to you in detail.

Chapter 4: Auctions and Dates

Lien and deed states function differently when it comes to their auctions. Technically, deed states don't have auctions - they have sales. The other difference is that deed sales happen more frequently than lien sales do. In fact, lien states have a large number of deed sales as well. This is because if the owner defaults on a lien, the investor has to recover their money by listing the property through a deed sale.

Typically, lien sales occur once every year. There's no pattern to which months of the year these auctions are held, so you should check with the local county's office or website for notices of the sale.

Government officials still advertise local lien sales in the dailies despite almost no one reading newspapers these days. This is a good thing because it means no one will know of these things occurring. If you're looking to keep reinvesting your money, you should plan a calendar of sales ahead of time.

This will help you identify potential auctions you could attend or bid at in case one of your liens is redeemed.

Fees

Much like how counties hold auctions at different times throughout the year, their fee structure is also different. Generally, the same structure holds throughout the state. However, larger counties (for example Los Angeles) might switch the rules a bit, thanks to high volumes.

No-Fee

The no-fee model is often followed by smaller counties. Their auctions aren't very well-attended and involve mostly rural properties. A typical lien auction for a small county might attract 10 people and the town's dog. The liens on offer might struggle to go higher than 50.

There are a few exceptions to this. Indianapolis is a large county but conducts no-fee auctions. The catch with no-fee auctions is that the winner is expected to pay the price of the lien immediately after the auction ends. Usually, the county cashier sits upfront and you'll be expected to pay using certified funds.

This can place a strain on investors. Some come equipped with cashier's checks and stick to a disciplined bidding strategy, so they don't exceed their budget. The same applies to online auctions as well. You'll be redirected to a payment gateway and will be expected to pay as soon as the auction ends.

Smaller counties might accept personal checks, but it's hit or miss. It's best to go equipped with a cashier's check or with a credit card in case of online payment.

Percentage Deposit

Certain counties ask you to enter the amount you plan on spending at the auction and ask you to deposit a percentage of that. This is typically 10% of your planned spend. If you happen to bid in such a way that your deposit dips under 10% of your spending, you'll be prompted to deposit more money before placing further bids.

These systems are prevalent online since it's impossible to track in person. If you're looking at spending a large amount of cash and don't want the system to lock you out thanks to dipping below the limit, you can deposit larger amounts (Lyons, 2020).

The deposit will be adjusted against your bids. If you happen to lose every bid, then you'll be refunded the entire amount. If your winning bids total less than the deposit, you'll be refunded the money via a check. This usually takes 10 business days to arrive in the mail.

Fixed Deposit

Larger counties that conduct in-person auctions use this method. Typically, the amount is $1,000, and it follows the same adjustment methods as mentioned in the section detailing the previous deposit method.

Smaller counties, mostly those in the Midwest, will charge smaller fees to the tune of $100 or $150 to allow you to take part in the auction. Some counties structure this as a fee, while others treat it as a deposit. So make sure you know how the counties you target treat this before registering for the auction.

Bidding Cards

Given that it's an auction, it stands to reason that the more cards you have at the event, the better your chances are of winning. Counties are up to speed on this, and limit the number of cards to one per person. When you register for the auction, you will need to provide your social security number along with the deposit payment.

You'll receive one card per social security number you register. If you have a corporation, you can acquire another card on its behalf. However, you'll be limited to carrying just one card into the auction hall. You can exit the room, swap your cards, and bid in that manner. However, in a live auction, each person can have just one card in play.

Experienced bidders hire people for a day or two and have them register as employees of their firm. Alternatively, they could bring a few family members along and have them bid. If the family member or employee wins the bid, they assign it to the investor. The county charges a small fee (around $20) per lien for this.

Assignment is as easy as checking a box at the bottom of the lien notice and filling in the name of the person it's being assigned to. Both parties sign the paper and file it with the county right after the auction ends, pay the fees, and that's it.

At smaller county sales, it isn't uncommon to find entire families bidding against you. There's a trade-off here. While the number of bidders is low, you'll be bidding against coordinated competition, so there's a chance you might not win the liens you have your eye on.

Larger auctions have more competition, but may be less coordinated, so you might end up winning more. However, given their popularity, the interest you earn might be lesser than what you might find at the smaller auctions.

Dates

If you're planning on being an active lien investor, you'll find that the way in which counties schedule their auction dates is inconvenient. For example, Iowa's counties typically hold all of their sales for around three or four days, once a year. This means you could find yourself switching between bidding online to driving to smaller counties at a rapid rate.

Even worse, a lot of these auctions are held at the same time of the day, so this puts the smaller investor at a disadvantage. While online systems have helped reduce this by a large degree, it can be confusing to track multiple auctions at once on your computer.

There are different types of auctions that take place, and you'll learn about this in the next chapter. However, switching from one auction to the next and switching auction types might cause confusion. It's best to plan a calendar for the year and approach these auctions in a structured manner.

Many states have moved their auctions entirely online so you don't have to worry about traveling anywhere. You could stick to these auctions, but attending the smaller, in-person auctions could lead to great deals. Registering online is pretty simple. You'll need to enter your social security number and pay the fees (except if it's a no-fee auction.)

Make sure you have funds lined up to pay for your winning bids. Typically, deposit-based auction counties give you two weeks to pay the balance on your winning bids. Some have more constricted timelines of 48 hours or even 24 hours. Make sure you understand the bidding process and procedures fully before participating. If you don't pay up, you'll forfeit your deposit and might even face a penalty in case your winning bid amounts are high (Kelley, 2020).

Online auctions aren't as exciting as in-person ones for obvious reasons. You'll enter your bid (which is the interest rate or the total lien amount depending on the type of auction) and sit back and wait. Once the bids are collected, the winning bid ticket is announced, and you'll receive a notification.

Online auctions also make it simpler for you to enter more cards in the auction. The registration method is the same. Simply have your related bidder enter their social security number and pay the deposit. It's best to stay away from bidding multiple cards on a single system, even if you're able to prevent yourself from being distracted.

Some of the larger counties frown upon such behavior and track IP addresses to crack down on it. It's best to use different devices when bidding in this way. It's even better to have them connected to different networks.

Another thing to keep in mind is that larger counties will require you to register in advance of the auction.

This is typically a week in advance. Smaller county auctions allow you to show up before the auction and register. Make sure you check the county's registration policy thoroughly.

Chapter 5: Bidding and Winning

With the advent of online auctions, the thrill of in-person auctions has largely receded. Larger counties these days conduct their auctions entirely online, and this means most investors don't have to attend large gatherings. This is a good thing for the new investor since in-person auctions can be extremely fast-paced and the chance of making an error is high.

If you do happen to attend an in-person auction, then it's best to sit quietly for a while until you get used to the flow of the event. In such auctions, hesitation or distraction can result in your losing out on a great deal. The county will publish the list of properties before the auction begins.

You should study the list of properties that are being auctioned off on a particular day. Some counties might work their way through the list in an orderly fashion while some might work off the listing numbers in ascending order. Either way, you'll have a list of properties that are coming onto the block, and should already have conducted basic due diligence on all of them.

I'll cover what kind of due diligence you need to

conduct in the next chapter. At the larger county auctions, you'll find that the majority of buyers will be institutional investors. Having said that, it isn't as if the CEO of a bank is going to come over and bid on these properties personally. The typical institutional investor is a college kid who has been hired on a temporary basis.

They get paid a few hundred bucks for a day's work and the institution gets a warm body to raise their cards and bid on the properties they want. These people usually have a list of properties that they're targeting, and are not allowed to stray from their target rates and properties. A consequence of this is if the county ends up auctioning properties that aren't on the published lists, you'll have no competition from these bidders.

A key part of bidding intelligently is to understand which type of auction you're taking part in. Let's take a look at these.

Bidding Systems

Before we get into the bidding systems, I must mention that county officials can elect to switch the bidding system midway through the auction. Some officials will even ignore the official system flat out. The state gives them the discretion to do this since the objective is to sell as many liens as possible.

If the county officer finds themselves falling behind schedule, you'll see them switch to a faster system.

Bid-Down

The most popular bid system is the bid-down. In this system, a statutory rate is declared and investors bid in lower amounts. The step size is usually a quarter percent. For example, if the statutory rate is 18%, the lower bid would be 17.75% and so on. I've written the number as a decimal but when yelling the number out loud, it's better to express it as a fraction. So you'd yell out "seventeen and three quarters" and so on.

If you find huge institutional interest in a property, then you'll likely find the interest rates crash almost immediately down to single digits. In the case of Florida's auctions, especially those in the larger counties, bids of a quarter percent are common. However, remember that these low bids are not always reflective of the true interest rate.

In Florida's case, the minimum interest rate paid is five percent. In addition to this, in case of default, a new lien is drawn and the statutory rate is paid until the deed is sold. If there are multiple bids that qualify as the lowest, the auctioneer picks one of the bids at random.

In online auctions, this is done through a random selection algorithm, so the process is completely fair. Online auctions are blind, which means officials cannot see who the entity is. Once the random winner is announced, the next lot is auctioned, and the process moves on.

Bid-down auctions are the ones that tend to be switched up the most in favor of other types of bidding. This is because a single lot takes time to be bid down. Counties have many properties to auction and, if they fall behind, the auctioneer moves to one of the other systems listed in this section.

There is no formal announcement of this happening. The official simply announces the lot in a different manner, which is in accordance to one of the other systems. As a final reminder, when bidding in this type of auction, remember that you're bidding on the interest rate. Some people think they're bidding on a fraction of the property's listing price or even worse, they think they're bidding on the actual price of the property. It's a bit unrealistic to think you'll acquire a million dollar property for "five", to say the least!

Premium Bidding

Premium bidding is one of the more confusing systems out there and a staggeringly large number of states use this system. The system works like this: Instead of bidding on an interest rate, investors shout out the total amount they would like to pay for the lien. If a lien is listed at $500, investors would shout $1,000 or $1,500 and so on.

A price of $1,500 indicates a premium of $1,000. Here's where it gets tricky. Counties treat the premium portion of the bid differently. There are five ways in which this is done (Cussen, 2020):

1. Interest is paid on both the price as well as the premium. Texas, for example, pays penalties on both amounts. This is the best and easiest system to understand.

2. Interest is paid at different rates on the price and premium. Indiana, for example, pays statutory rates on the price but pays a lower rate of simple interest on the premium.
3. Interest is paid only on the price and not the premium. Premium is returned once the lien is redeemed.
4. Interest is paid only on the premium and not on the lien price. Both amounts are returned to the investor upon redemption.
5. Premium is lost. Interest is paid only on the lien and only the lien amount is returned on redemption.

Methods two through six require the investor adjust their bids according to the interest they wish to receive. For example, if an investor wishes to receive five percent returns on an investment of $1,000 in an auction that is employing method number three, they can bid on liens up to $500 at 10% interest.

This represents a premium of $500, and they'll receive $50 as interest. This equates to five percent returns on their total investment.

A few small counties have an odd system of bidding. Instead of the auctioneer announcing the lot under auction, they'll list the lot numbers on a screen and investors can shout out the number they're interested in. The other investors then raise their cards once someone shouts out a number indicating their interest in it along with their bid. This proceeds until the auctioneer announces the winning bid.

Random Selection

This isn't an official bidding method, but it's one that auctioneers resort to when they wish to speed things up. If there are a small number of bidders in the room, the auctioneer will typically ask a random bidder if they want a lien. If that person declines, they move on to another person, and the next, until the lien finds a bidder.

If no one wants the lien, the auctioneer announces that the lien is up for bidding and if it still doesn't find a bidder, they move onto the next one. As you can see, this method works best when there are a few people in the room. At bid-down auctions, you'll find this method being used during the times when there's a lull in proceedings; for example, when investors have left the room for lunch.

Some auctions carry on beyond their announced end times, and you'll find random selection being used then as well. At smaller counties, you'll find the bid numbers written on ping pong balls and loaded into a bucket. The auctioneer picks a number at random and offers the lien to them.

Rotational Bidding

This is a method that is the fairest to all bidders. However, this only means that it leaves everyone equally dissatisfied. The auctioneer begins with the first lot and offers it to the first bidder on the list and works their way down until the lot is taken. Then the second lot is offered to the second bidder first, and the entire list is worked through in this manner.

This means everyone receives a chance to accept a property. The bad news is that you have no idea which property you're going to be offered. You might be offered a dismal one or something that is far too expensive. The consolation is that at least you'll be offered a fair chance.

Since there's no bidding, this method is used in states that offer a fixed interest rate on liens. Iowa, for example, uses this method at the beginning of the auctions at smaller counties before resorting to the previous method (in case things need to be sped up).

Ownership Bid-Down

This method makes the least sense and is, thankfully, almost non-existent. The idea is that investors bid down the amount of the property they wish to encumber with the lien. For example, if a lot is announced, the investor can shout out 90%. This means they'll own the lien at the price advertised, but this will cover just 90% of the entire property.

This makes no sense at all since enforcing this in court is possible only if there's another lien to account for the 10%, and if both lien owners are in agreement as to how to proceed. The good news is that while there are some states that officially announce the use of this method, few actually practice it.

For example, Nebraska officially uses this bidding method but resorts to a bid-down system in reality. Online auctions using this system default to a rotational bid, premium, or a bid-down most of the time. One wonders why the ownership bid-down system was even conceived to begin with.

OTC

OTC stands for "over the counter" and is technically not a bidding method. Once auctions end, there are always liens that are left unsold. This happens either because the auctioneer couldn't get through their full list, or that the investor could not pay the amount required to purchase the lien.

Every in-person auction has instances where miscommunication occurs and the investor bids on a property other than the one they're interested in. In such cases, the county allows for the sale to be annulled and the lien goes back into the pile. Thanks to many liens being present, the sold-and-unsold lien goes back to the bottom of the pile.

Visit the county's office to inquire about the liens that have been left unsold. You can purchase them right away for their face value and you will receive the statutory interest rate since there's no bidding involved. Liens sold this way are usually marked "private sale" by the county, indicating that it wasn't bought at an auction. There are no repercussions to liens being sold this way - it's just a method of record the county uses.

Tips

Most of these tips will cover physical auctions. Online auctions don't produce the same level of emotions, and beginner investors find them easier to deal with.

Go Small

A typical problem investors face is that they cannot compete with institutional investors. They find great properties being bid down to low rates of return, and this causes consternation. One way of avoiding institutional interest is to bid on smaller liens. Institutions have millions of dollars to invest.

As a result, they need properties of a certain size to be able to earn attractive rates of return. This means a lien worth $1,000 isn't going to move the needle. A $20 return on $1,000 equals a 0.02% return on a million dollar portfolio. That's less than the rate at which banks can borrow money from the government.

Therefore, seek to accumulate smaller liens, and build your portfolio that way instead of chasing large properties. Over time, once you build your own roll up significantly, you can go after those large properties.

Sticking with the going small theme, attending auctions at smaller counties often works better for beginner investors. Banks and institutions need to be able to market their properties in case the owners fail to redeem their liens. This means that they need properties situated in attractive areas where there's a lot of demand.

This leaves small towns and counties relatively competition-free for you. I'm not implying that you'll gain hugely attractive bargains. It's just that your competitors will be other small investors and not banks.

Pay Attention to the Property

Institutions are after certain types of properties. These are typically residential properties or commercially-viable ones. Properties such as gas stations or homes in less desirable areas are not what they're after. Every once in a while, you'll end up seeing high-value properties that go for high rates because the institutions stay away from them.

Remain Alert

This one applies to in-person auctions. Auctioneers are looking to move through their list of liens quickly. You'll find that they won't pause for more than a second or so after a bid is announced. If you happen to have an interest in the property, then bid as quickly as you can and keep following the bid.

This is daunting for beginners because the pace of auctions can take everyone by surprise. However, observe the room when you first walk in and soak it up. This will allow you to adjust to the pace of the auction and you'll find yourself bidding like a pro in no time.

Target Lulls

Auctions happen throughout the day and people show up for them at six in the morning. The official times are often from nine to five, but institutions often send their people early to capture the best seats in the house. As a result, as noon rolls around, everyone's exhausted and hungry for some food.

The hours between midday and 1 P.M. are when you'll witness an exodus from the auction hall. This is also when you stand to score some real bargains without the pressure of institutional competition. Stick around during these times, and also during the last hours of the auction.

Often, auctions run over their allotted time and you'll find that institutional bidders will leave after 5 P.M. These times are when county officials will auction properties that aren't on the published lists, so sticking around can help you score some great deals. If they aren't published, the institutions haven't conducted due diligence on them, and as a result, they won't bid on them. This is a massive win for you!

Hang Onto Your Card

This is a big one. County officials cannot be expected to remember everyone's names. Your bid number is all they have to go by. Misplace your card or lose it and you'll have a real headache on your hands. The worst-case scenario is if someone else picks it up and mistakenly bids using your number.

This closes our look at the bidding process. You might be wondering what happens if the owner doesn't redeem their lien? This is what the next chapter deals with.

Chapter 6: Foreclosure and Securing Your Investment

Tax liens will usually be redeemed before their redemption period ends, but there is a significant possibility that the property's owner will default on their payment. This can happen for as many reasons as you can imagine. Perhaps they're forced into bankruptcy, or they might happen to be out-of-country owners for whom the hassle of owning the property isn't worth it anymore.

When this happens, the tax lien investor stands to acquire the property free and clear. Much like how there are different bidding types at in-person auctions, there are two primary methods by which states handle such situations.

The first and easiest method to understand is the filing method. Before getting into that, it's worth revisiting the biggest advantage of tax lien investing. A tax lien is the senior debt when it comes to existing liens on a property. If the property has two mortgages on it, the tax lien supersedes both of them.

Tax Liens And Deeds Investing

If you move to foreclose the property, the owners of the mortgage debt will be wiped out. This is why banks invest in both the mortgages and on the liens attached to the property. Buying the lien simply secures their investment. Often, you'll find that the tax lien payment is in default but the mortgages are not. What happens in this case?

Since the tax lien is senior to a mortgage, you can still move to foreclose the property. In real life, the mortgage owner will be aware of the redemption period of the lien and will pay you the outstanding amount to avoid foreclosure. After all, if they don't do this, they'll lose their investment in the property.

Often, investors look at the relative sizes of the tax lien amount and the mortgage and conclude that the mortgage must be senior. For example, if the outstanding tax lien is $5,000 and the mortgage is $200,000, they think the mortgage is senior because it's a larger debt.

This is not the case at all. For the price of $5,000 you can end up owning the entire property and remove the mortgage holder from contention. This is why some alternative forms of real estate investment, such as mortgage notes investing, are fraught with risk. Those investments are pushed as being risk-free, since they involve buying mortgages. However, mortgages are lower on the priority scale when compared to property tax liens. The only lien that is senior to a tax lien is an earlier tax lien or any other lien placed by the county for its services. A property tax lien that is even a day older than your lien will be senior to yours.

If this is the case, you'll have to pay the holder of the first lien before you can assume the senior-most position. If redemption periods last for multiple years, each year counts as a separate lien. For example, if you buy a lien whose principal is $2,500 and if the redemption period is three years, there will be three liens on the property and you'll own all of them.

So now that you understand how advantageous tax liens can be, let's look at the filing process for foreclosure. This is one of two methods that states use to initiate proceedings.

Filing for Foreclosure

Once the property owner has defaulted on their payment and when the redemption period has passed, you can head over to the county office and file your intention to foreclose on the property. This is a simple process whereby you'll fill out some paperwork, pay an administrative fee and file a notice to the property owner.

In most cases, you can post a legal notice in a designated newspaper as well for a period of a week. If the owner does not respond to these notices and if they don't clear their payment, you own the property free and clear.

It sounds incongruous to think that you could own a $100,000 property for an investment of $2,500, but this is precisely what happens when you foreclose. Most tax lien states operate in this manner. I must mention that such occurrences don't happen frequently for the individual investor.

This is because such properties are typically bid down at the auction by institutions. The remaining pile of properties is distributed between vacant lots in undesirable areas or properties that require considerable repair. You might get lucky every once in a while, but it's best to avoid investing in liens with the intention of acquiring the property.

Look at tax lien investing as something that brings you steady cash flow and consider foreclosing on a property as being a bonus that occurs once in a while. Once you own the property, you're free to do what you want with it. If it has tenants you can continue to lease it to them and earn rental income. If this happens, you'll earn a significant return on your investment.

More often than not, tax lien investors end up selling the property to rehabbers or home flippers. Due to the initial investment being low, selling at below market rates results in a huge gain. Imagine acquiring a property for a total investment of $3,000 to $5,000 and then selling the property for $50,000 in an area where the average home sells for $70,000.

I must mention that you'll have to clear any senior liens on the property before you can foreclose. This payment is typically made on the same day as when you visit the county office to fill out any paperwork. What happens if you're the junior tax lien? In this case, you can approach the owner of the senior lien and offer to buy them out.

If they refuse, unfortunately, then you have no other option but to forego your investment. This is why it's important to research on whether there are existing tax liens on the property before you bid for a property.

Tax Deed Foreclosures

The second type of foreclosure involves a tax deed sale. I've mentioned this in passing previously. In a tax deed foreclosure state, the initial steps you'll take are the same as with a filing state. You'll head over to the county office and fill out paperwork. Once this is done though, the county handles all notices.

They'll notify the owner as well as publish legal notices of a tax deed sale occurring. This happens three or four months after the foreclosure filing is made. During this time, you'll be paid the statutory rate the state pays on liens. For example, Florida will pay you 18% during this time.

Another thing to keep in mind is that, during this period, the owner has the option to step in and clear their lien. If they do this, the foreclosure is cancelled. The owners of the junior liens can also step in and compensate you for the lien. Whether you choose to accept this or not is up to you.

Typically, investors will accept a premium from the mortgage holders depending on the property. If the mortgage is held by a private investor, you can structure a deal in any way you want. It's possible to get creative here and work out a deal that gives you a portion of the cash flow and some kind of joint ownership. If it's your first time doing this, then it's best to keep it simple. Simply proceed with the foreclosure or wait for the owner to redeem you. You'll be paid to wait (via interest), so it's not as if you're losing anything.

If the owner doesn't step in during this period, the property goes to a tax deed sale. Deed sales are a little known but highly lucrative method for property investors to acquire lots for pennies on the dollar. Foreclosures and bank-owned property sales get all the attention but deed sales witness greater discounts.

The flip side is that the kinds of properties that reach a deed sale aren't always the most desirable. As a result, only experienced investors attend them since they'll need to quickly evaluate how much money the investment will truly cost. As a lien investor, you don't need to worry about any of this.

During the sale, you'll be guaranteed compensation to the tune of your investment in the lien. If no one bids an amount that is equal to or greater than your investment, you'll own the property free and clear. If someone does bid an amount greater than your lien investment, they'll own the property and you'll be compensated according to the principal and interest rate governing the lien.

The bottom line is that, whatever happens, you'll receive your money back. You can also stand to own the property as a bonus. In reality, most tax deed sales result in the lien owner being compensated and someone else receiving the property. You can participate in the deed sale if you wish and join in the bidding.

Chapter 7: Risks and What to Watch for

Tax lien investing is great but there are some risks to it that you must watch out for. This chapter will bring you up to speed on all of them.

Internal Revenue Service Liens

There's no escaping the IRS. Some properties might have an IRS tax lien on them. There are a lot of misconceptions surrounding how this works, so let me make this clear. Irrespective of the state you're investing in, the IRS lien is equal to yours.

Once the redemption period ends, and if the property is in default, the IRS has 120 days to buy you out. The disadvantage is that the IRS will redeem you at a standard rate of six percent interest from the date you purchased the lien. If you purchased the lien at 15%, you'll receive just six.

In addition to this, the IRS will also pay you any expenses associated with the process. Thus, you're protected even if the IRS owns a lien on the property. It's just that you'll have to wait an additional 120 days after the default occurs for them to respond. If they do, your risk is that you'll receive six percent interest.

If they don't respond, you can proceed to foreclose on the property. The bottom line is that the IRS lien isn't senior to yours. You're equal.

Owner Bankruptcy

This doesn't happen too often but when it does, it poses a few risks. If the owner files for bankruptcy before the redemption period ends, the judge assigned to the case suspends all claims against the owner. This means your lien's payment will be delayed. There are other wrinkles that can occur.

The judge might order your lien to be repaid in full at the interest rate that you've secured in the bidding after the sale of the property. However, they might even state that all creditors will be paid pennies on the dollar. There's nothing you can do in such scenarios (Lyons, 2020).

In some cases, you'll find that the owner will name all of their creditors in their petition. This means that you'll have to file an answer with the court confirming your claim. This requires the services of an attorney. If your investment was a few hundred dollars, it's not worth it to pursue this claim.

There isn't a clear way to avoid the risk of bankruptcy proceedings affecting your investment. The best thing to do is to bid on higher value liens. A tax lien usually represents around two percent of the property's value. If you've bought a lien worth $3,000, the property is worth $150,000.

Higher-priced property owners are less likely to file for bankruptcy. This doesn't mean you'll never have to deal with it. It just reduces the odds of it.

Worthless Lots

This is the biggest risk to the tax lien investor. County officials are primarily concerned with collecting taxes.

They couldn't care less about the type of property that they're offering. As a result, you could end up owning liens on a property that no one has any interest in.

For example, vacant properties that are too small to build on, or ones located next to a power line or substation are considered worthless. The owner of the property will not redeem and you'll end up owning a piece of land that you can't do anything with.

The best way to avoid these situations is to stay away from lots priced under $1,000. The downside is that these tiny investment sizes offer the highest yields, often well above 20% in states where the statutory rate is high.

Another option you have is to bid only on homestead properties. These are properties that are occupied and are the primary residence of the occupier. This makes it certain that the property is a good one. The rates of return will be low but you're assured a safe return for a large dollar amount.

Some counties will be nice enough to list pictures of the property online - however most won't. You can stick to bidding in areas you're familiar with to avoid bidding on a worthless lot. Alternatively, you can check the lot listings on the county's website and type the address into Google's street view. This will allow you to take a quick look at what the property is.

If you don't know what a property is and if the dollar amount is below $1,000, stay away from it.

Early Redemption

This is the second-largest risk that lien investors face. If the redemption period is one year and if the owner redeems after a month, you're going to receive a fraction of the interest rate you bid. Some states recognize this risk and offer penalty rates in cases of early redemption. For example, Florida's penalty rate is five percent, as explained earlier.

This means you'll receive a return of five percent no matter what. However, some states don't offer this. Iowa offers a two percent return per month for 24% returns per year. This is pretty great. However, if the owner redeems after a month, you'll receive just a two percent payment on your principal.

You'll now need to find other avenues of investment for your money. Most investors don't worry about this, but it does increase the amount of work you'll need to carry out.

Chapter 8: Tax Deeds

It's now time to enter the realm of tax deed auctions. You've already learned that roughly half the states in America follow the lien system with the other half following the deed system, and with 10 states following a hybrid system. Keep in mind that despite some states such as New York and Ohio being deed states, they do tend to auction liens in certain counties.

In Ohio's case, counties with populations greater than 200,000 can sell liens. The way these liens work is the same as detailed previously, so there's no additional knowledge you need. All you have to do is check with the county registrar whether they sell liens or not.

Deed investing is a bit different in that you'll now own the property outright instead of a lien on it. It's a more direct form of real estate investment and requires you to have cash in the bank. In case you're wondering, most lenders don't issue mortgages against a tax deed since it isn't equivalent to a title.

The process also changes a bit in the case of hybrid states, which makes the possibility of obtaining financing difficult.

Hybrid States

Texas and Georgia are perfect examples of hybrid states, and it's instructive to examine how they execute the process. Once the deed is sold, the investor owns the property - however the prior owner still has the chance to redeem. The redemption period depends on the type of property you've bought.

Non-homestead and non-agricultural properties have redemption periods of six months. Truth be told, most of these properties are unlikely to be redeemed. Consider that Texas has a penalty rate of 25%. Over and above this, the property's previous owner has to cough up their property taxes.

Next, in order to get the property back from you, they need to pay you whatever you paid to buy the property. Lastly, they need to pay any fines that the county assesses on them. Over and above this, they need to pay 25% of all this as a penalty! Coughing up this much money in six months is close to impossible.

Homestead and agricultural properties have a two-year redemption period. The options that the previous owner has are the same, in that they'll need to compensate you to the tune of 25% per year on your investment. Given the length of time, it's possible that the previous owner might compensate you. However, since the property is in default in the first place, it's unlikely.

Something that deed investors do quite often is to rent the place out in order to boost their returns on the investment. You might not want to carry out large-scale repairs due to the redemption option being available to the previous owner, but you can give it a new coat of paint and change the door handles and so on.

Remember that this process is how it works in hybrid states. States that are outright deed states (listed below) will not offer the previous owner any redemption option. It isn't as if the county will arbitrarily push the property into an auction upon default. The property's owner will have ample notice to the tune of at least two years.

The county will post notices to the owner throughout this time, so it isn't as if they'll be blindsided by it.

Deed States

Here are the states that are purely deed states:

- Alaska
- Arkansas
- California
- Idaho
- Kansas
- Maine
- Michigan
- Minnesota
- Nevada
- New Hampshire
- New Mexico
- New York
- North Carolina
- Ohio
- Oregon
- Pennsylvania
- Utah
- Virginia
- Washington

Pennsylvania can conduct lien sales if the property has been occupied continuously for 90 days prior to the deed auction. Ohio allows liens to be sold in counties with populations greater than 200,000. In addition to this, New York also conducts lien auctions in a few counties.

Pros and Cons

Just as with tax lien investing, there are advantages and disadvantages to the tax deed investing process.

Pros

The biggest advantage of an outright tax deed purchase is that you own the property in full. Usually, you won't have to worry about any senior liens on the property. At most, the county might impose a maintenance lien for the work they carried out to make it inhabitable.

Thanks to this, you don't have to wait for the redemption period to end and neither do you need to worry about early redemptions. Since you own the property, you're free to do whatever you want with it and this allows you to take advantage of other methods of real estate investment.

The most common type of tax deed investor is the home flipper. The properties that are offered at tax deed sales tend to require some form of work, and this presents huge opportunities for this type of investor. Also, unlike tax lien investing, counties will provide full listings and property information prior to a tax deed sale.

You might see counties slip a few listings in during tax lien sales that they didn't disclose previously, thanks to the large volume of liens present. This does not happen with tax deed auctions.

In addition to this, the number of tax deed auctions that take place are far greater than liens. Lien auctions occur in a county once a year, but deed auctions take place all the time. This is the case even in full-lien states. This gives investors more opportunity to purchase a property for pennies on the dollar.

As I mentioned earlier, deed auctions provide greater bargains than foreclosure sales provide. This is mainly because counties are primarily interested in recovering their taxes. Unlike a bank that conducts an auction, they aren't worried about the purchase price of their investment.

This means that bidding usually starts at the amount owed on taxes and goes up from there. The typical tax deed auction results in properties selling for 10-60 cents on the dollar as opposed to 50-80 cents in foreclosures and REO sales. There is the possibility of the property being bid to a premium, of course, but such instances are rare.

Cons

The reason most properties in tax deed auctions sell for so little has to do with the fact that they aren't very desirable. I'll cover this in more detail shortly, but you're not going to find too many gems in here. Some investors go into these thinking they'll unearth a million dollar property for a few thousands, but this just isn't the case.

For the most part, you'll also be competing with seasoned real estate investors and will need to make snap judgements during the auction. The dollar amount of investment required is also a lot higher. After all, you're acquiring a property and not just a lien. This means you'll need around $40,000 and above to even think about bidding.

The higher the dollar amount you're able to invest, the more tax deed auctions will make sense for you. Good properties will sell for high-five to low-six figures. Not everyone has that kind of money in cash except for seasoned real estate investors. Some investors work with a hard money lender to obtain financing, but unless you have a strong relationship with one of them, you're unlikely to obtain such financing.

There's also the fact that most of these properties will require rehab work. You're free to inspect the property, but you're not going to be able to conduct a thorough appraisal with your contractor. This means you'll have to eyeball the damage and estimate repair costs. You can allow a margin of safety in your calculations, but this might not always be adequate.

All of this means that tax deed investing is for more experienced and well-heeled investors. This doesn't mean beginners cannot profit from them, but you need to really do your homework before attempting to purchase a property.

Types of Properties

Tax Liens And Deeds Investing

So what kinds of properties show up on tax deed auctions? Technically speaking, anything can show up - from commercial property to residential to vacant lots. In reality, it's mostly rundown residential or commercial property or odd-sized vacant lots. This might sound terrible at first glance, but there's always value to be had in such properties.

While you obviously will want to stay away from smaller vacant lots, you can make money buying or rehabbing some of the larger properties on offer. As a rule of thumb, you must expect to invest even more money into the property for rehab work. The exact amount of money you'll need to invest is impossible to estimate, since so much depends on the nature of the repairs you'll need to carry out.

However, you should have some cash on hand to account for these. Given the high dollar amounts in question, it's important for you to correctly estimate the maximum amount you can bid, along with knowing the factors that govern the value of the property in question.

As a rule of thumb, it's best to stick to your local area, or an area of expertise when bidding at a deed auction. This won't be a problem, since there will be many deeds being auctioned in your area. It isn't like tax liens, where you'll have just one day during a year to take full advantage and invest your money.

Is it possible for a really good property to be auctioned? It is, but it's best to not expect something like this to fall into your lap. Good properties aren't usually in a defaulted state, and their owners will do their best to hang onto them. It's more likely you'll find good properties making their way into tax lien auctions than deed auctions.

Of course, even with lien investing, you'll find that the owners will redeem you quickly. Deed investing requires you to let go of thoughts of finding properties that are extremely desirable. A lot of this type of investing requires you to identify opportunities in properties that the average person looks at with a jaundiced eye.

Chapter 9: Scoring Bargains and Avoiding Bad Investments

One of the reasons most investors get into deed investing is to score bargains. Is it possible to score pennies on the dollar? It's possible, but improbable. For the most part, you'll see auction values of 50 cents on the dollar. Still, this is a pretty good investment by itself and represents the possibility of a tidy profit.

However, there are many ways you can increase your odds of scoring a steal. The most obvious way is to attend deed auctions once the redemption period on a lien has expired. These auctions witness little competition for a few reasons. For starters, the county does not go out of its way to advertise this auction.

For the most part, the only ones receiving notices are the lien holders and other investors who make it a point to read obscure legal notices in newspapers. No one else reads these announcements in the newspapers, so you can imagine the number of people who'll show up. Since your investment in a lien is extremely low (in comparison to the property's value) you might end up with a real gem on your hands.

As a rule of thumb, counties assess the value of properties at 80% of their market value. However, this doesn't mean every property will conform to this. Property values are set by the county assessor's office and the employees are typically in another location. All they have to go by is the value of adjacent properties.

This leads to smaller, worthless lots, according to the market, being priced the same as adjacent lots. You should take care and stay away from such properties at all costs. What are the odds of you scoring a steal at tax lien auctions? Truth be told, quite low.

If the property is a good one, the odds of an owner letting it go for back taxes is quite low. Put yourself in their shoes: Would you let your million-dollar property go for an amount equivalent to two percent of its value? Thus, the best approach at such auctions is to hope for the best and not expect gems to drop in your lap. If one does fall into your lap, then this is a bonus.

Vacant Lots

Vacant lots are a double-edged sword. You can find real gems here but you're also going to unearth a ton of stinkers. The problem with vacant lots is that they're often assessed at unrealistic values. I've just explained why this is so. If the value of the property is unfair, you're not going to have many options in terms of recourse.

You could try to fight the case in the courts, but in terms of priorities, it's going to rank pretty low. Besides, the county might just decide to hit you with the tax anyway. Generally speaking, it's not worth pursuing this option.

A lot of vacant lot investing is speculative. For example, you might find a vacant lot available many miles outside a large metropolitan area. You could buy this plot in the hopes of someone buying it down the road. Either way, it won't cost you too much, so it's worth an investment.

You'll often see vacant lots advertised for values that are nowhere near their true market value. Needless to say, it's best to stay away from such properties. You'll need to conduct thorough research prior to bidding on such properties. Often, counties will have different laws that will dictate building guidelines.

For example, if you buy a land that is 55 feet wide, you won't be able to build anything on it if the county specifies that the minimum width ought to be 57 feet. Keep these requirements in mind at all times. As long as you're aware of them, you'll find that scoring bargains on vacant lots is a realistic way of owning property for very little upfront investment.

Rehabs

These are a pretty common sight at a deed auction. The trick is to bid prices that make sense for you. Often, you'll find these coming up for sale during lien auctions as well and, in case the owner doesn't redeem it, you could consider bidding for the property at the subsequent deed auction.

The biggest issue is that you'll need to estimate for after repair values (ARV) and repair costs. Furthermore, it's impossible to be an out-of-state rehabber since you'll need to devote a lot of time to inspecting the place and arranging tasks with your contractors. As a result, the world of opportunity you'll have with it will be low.

This doesn't mean you cannot invest in such properties, though. If you manage to score a bargain that is well below the average market price, you could earn up to 50% returns on the purchase. For example, if you end up owning a property for $5,000 in an area where the average price is $50,000, you could sell the property for $10,000 to a rehabber and earn a tidy profit on your investment.

More often than not, such properties will be present in less desirable areas of town. This means you'll have to be careful when it comes to vetting the property. Most lien investors stay away from these kinds of properties, especially if they're vacant and boarded up.

However, you could bid on them at the eventual deed auction with a view towards long-term investment. Who knows what the area will look like 20 years down the road? Besides, governments are quite keen on rehabilitating decrepit parts of town and sometimes offer many schemes and subsidies to property owners in these places.

If there is such a program running, you could take advantage of it and boost your investment's return.

Minimum Bid Research

This one's a bit off the beaten track. Most counties fix the minimum bid at a deed auction to be equal to the liens owed on it. For example, if the property's assessed worth is $80,000, and if the outstanding liens are worth $1,600, the minimum bid will be $1,600.

However, not all counties do this. Some smaller counties have minimums as low as $100 despite the amount of taxes owed on the property. In such cases, the county is willing to forego the taxes on the property - either because it doesn't make a dent in their budget or because it just isn't worth it.

The exact reasons are irrelevant. As far as you're concerned, all that matters is that the asking price is extremely low and you can stand to score a real bargain if there isn't much competition for the property at the auction. Some counties in Kansas, for example, have minimum bids for as low as 50 cents (Lyons, 2020).

If you're serious about seeking huge bargains, then sticking to such counties makes sense. Keep in mind that the property type also plays an important role.

You could score a "bargain" on a completely worthless property as well. So do not skimp on the due diligence you conduct prior to the auction. A low selling price doesn't indicate a bargain, however, in and of itself.

Avoiding Risks

The risks are higher when investing in deeds (compared to liens), thanks to the dollar amount involved in the purchase. This means you'll need to conduct your due diligence on the properties thoroughly. Here are some of the risks you'll face when dealing with deed auction properties and how you can avoid them.

Non-Existent Properties

This sounds like something I'm making up but it occurs more often than you think. Here's why this occurs. When a developer files paperwork with the county, they need to notify them of the exact details of the property involved. For example, if they're developing a group of condos, they'll need to specify the number of units in the building and their dimensions.

However, property development is a complex business. If the developer runs out of funds or if some other issue is uncovered, plans change. Let's say some of those units that were in the original filing end up not being built. The developer files notice of these architectural changes with the county.

Given the way typical government offices work, though, there's no guarantee that these changes will be appended to the original filing. The department that deals with these permits might attach them, but the assessor's office might not see them. As a result, the county believes there are, say, 10 units in the complex, while the developer has built just nine.

What happens to this phantom 10th unit? It goes to auction! This happens in both lien and deed states, by the way. With a lien state, you can avoid it by looking at either the lien value or the vacancy status. Besides, the dollar amount is a lot lower and while it'll hurt to lose money, you're not going to lose too much of your capital.

However, with deeds, it's a different matter altogether. If an average condo is selling for $100,000, you're going to be out-of-pocket for that amount and will face years fighting a legal battle against the county.

To avoid such situations, always visit the property personally. Do not consider bidding unless you've set your two feet on the property premises and have taken a look at it. Anything else, even online views, should not count.

Environmental Issues

This tends to happen with vacant lots or lots adjacent to industrial zones. It's not a very common issue but when it does occur, you'll have a real headache on your hands. For their part, county officials are diligent in this regard and will append a note that explains the existence of any environmental issues.

Most investors stay away from these properties for obvious reasons. If you happen to have inside knowledge on the specific type of problem that's afflicting the site, then you can bid on it and score a steal. However, most investors don't fall into this category, so it's best they stay away from such properties.

Sometimes, you'll have environmental issues crop up after buying the property. This can be the case with land that has been zoned for industrial use. The best way to avoid these properties is to view it in person. You'll be able to figure out what the issue is firsthand.

Next, stay away from gas stations or properties adjacent to them. These places produce a lot of waste that you'll be liable to dispose ethically and this costs a lot of money. If you happen to be aware of the nature of the problem and can handle it, then invest in it by all means.

If you happen to be a beginner investor, though, it's best to stick to residential vacant land, residential properties and commercial properties. Build your experience in these areas and then adopt more risk later on.

IRS Liens

You've already learned how IRS liens work and the 120-day delay they impose on you. When it comes to tax lien investing, there isn't too much risk in buying properties with IRS liens on them. At worst, you'll receive a lower interest rate.

However, when it comes to deed investing, the risks are high. For starters, you'll have to wait for 120 days to see a return on your investment and you can't do anything with the property until this window passes. You'll also need the assistance of an attorney in case the IRS does decide to redeem the property.

It's best to steer clear of such situations. The county will release a list of lot numbers that have IRS liens placed on them. Avoiding them is as easy as not bidding on any property that's on that list.

Chapter 10: Mastering the Auction

The auction process that accompanies tax deed sales is pretty straightforward. Unlike with lien investing where you'll have to contend with different bidding types, with deeds, it's as simple as bidding the highest price. This brings with it its own problems, of course.

Auctions are designed to garner the highest price possible for an asset. The county's objective is to gain as high a price as possible for the property, and they don't fool around when it comes to this. Most counties hire professional auctioneers to conduct auctions and you'll find that the pace conducted will be fast.

This chapter is going to give you a few tips to stay ahead of the game and also a few things you need to watch out for.

Research

A lot of mistakes that occur at auctions emanate from the investor not conducting their due diligence beforehand. Keep in mind that the majority of investors present at these auctions will be experienced people. There might be a few rookies around, but for the most part, people here know what they're doing.

You don't want to be that person who makes mistakes that could have been avoided entirely. Here's a step-by-step method you can use to conduct due diligence prior to the auction.

Step One - Check The Property File

This is an obvious step, really. Visit the county office or their website to look at the property file. This will be a sizable document and will contain all information about the property, including taxes owed. It'll also list the nature of the property, whether it's a vacant lot or has a structure on it. The relevant zone of the property will also be listed.

Typically, occupied properties will be cleared before the deed sale. Make a note of these properties for later use. This will save you a lot of time in the following steps. Something that first-time investors ignore is to take a look at the percentage of taxes owed against the property's value.

Some counties auction properties that have over 10 years' worth of taxes owed on them. This means the liens will amount to 20% of the total property value or more (property taxes are around two percent of the total value). As a rule of thumb, you want to stay below this percentage figure. Go above this and you'll stand a smaller chance of getting a deep bargain.

Note the fees and costs associated with the process as well. The county will list these quite prominently.

Step Two - Check Comps

A "comp" is short for "comparable". A comparable in turn is a sale of a property that occurred recently, one that closely matches the type of property you're looking at. There's an art to evaluating comps and it's something that experienced investors tend to be good at.

For starters, you might get lucky and find a similar property that sold in the same neighborhood. Let's say beginner's luck doesn't assist you, and that you find nothing comparable in the area. What do you do now?

One method is to look at the sales on a per-square-foot basis or on a per-bedroom basis. For example, if the property you're looking at is a one-bedroom home, and the only comparable has three bedrooms that sold in the past six months, you can divide the sale price according to the number of bedrooms the house has. This will give you a rough figure.

A common scenario is the lack of comps within six months of the deed auction date. If nothing in the area has sold over this time, then you're going to have to cast a wider net. You could expand your comp search to a year. These prices won't be as accurate but it will get you in the ballpark.

If you find no comps in this timeframe, you'll need to look for comps in a wider radius from your property's location. A common radius to use initially is three miles. If this doesn't give you any comps, then expand it to six miles. If even this doesn't give you any comps, expand to 10 miles.

This usually does the trick. If you're out of luck and still can't find anything, you can visit a local realtor's office and check prices. Alternatively, you can take a look at sale listings currently in the area online through websites such as Zillow or Roofstock. In the case of vacant land, this won't be a viable option.

Instead, you should visit the local realtor's office and make inquiries. Of course, this process is a whole lot easier if you're operating close to your own neighborhood. Asking around in your local real estate investment club is also a good option. If you're out of state, looking up local realtors is the best way forward.

The point of this exercise, in case it isn't obvious, is to determine the approximate market value of the property you're planning on bidding for.

Step Three - Locate

This one applies solely to vacant lots. Counties will typically not list the street address of a vacant lot. Instead, it'll be a mish-mash of which property the one you're looking at is next to. Counties will have plat maps you can use to locate exactly where the land is located.

Step Four - Visit

This is self-explanatory. You should always visit the property in question before an auction. I'll shortly address the timeline for property visits. When visiting a property, make sure you take a lot of photos. This is especially the case if the property in question requires you to rehab it in order to sell it for a profit.

You can use these pictures along with detailed notes and run it past a contractor for an initial estimate. They won't be able to give you a final cost but it can help you figure out how much you'll need to allocate for a fix and flip.

The property visit is also where you should nail down the maximum price you're willing to bid for it. Having this in place is crucial. The auction environment encourages competition, and in the drive to win, we might end up forgetting how much we can truly afford. Fix a maximum price and stick to it no matter what.

A good way of fixing this is to look for the kind of return you want from the property. You might want a 90% margin on the property which will require you to bid at 10 cents on the dollar. Generally speaking, vacant land can sell for these rates. It's more realistic to expect 25 cents.

Properties that need rehab work generally go for 50 cents on the dollar or even 70 cents if the rehab costs are low. The more expensive a property is, the lower its auction price will be since these properties will require significant investment.

Step Five - Time Your Visits

Your time is important and you should minimize wasting it. To this end, you need to schedule your property visits in an ordered manner. It's good practice to visit the properties in question not more than two business days prior to the auction. This might seem like a tight timeline. Let me explain.

If the auction is on a Friday, then you should visit properties on the Wednesday and Thursday prior to it. Why is this? Put simply, most properties will redeem before the auction begins. The last thing you want to be doing is to waste time looking at properties that won't be present when the auction starts.

Once you become more experienced, you can schedule your visits a day before the auction. Use the day before that to visit the county office and gather preliminary information. By placing your site visits as close to the auction as possible, you'll use your time more efficiently.

Tips for Success

I've already discussed a few tips for succeeding at auctions. Even though those were for tax liens, an auction is an auction. Those tips apply equally for tax deeds. Here are a few additional tips for you to keep in mind.

Stick to Your Maximum

This is something that is easy to forget in the frenzy that accompanies bidding. Much like tax lien auctions, you'll find that deed auctions progress at a breakneck pace. Except here, the dollar amounts are a lot bigger.

Hence, you need to be even more disciplined when it comes to bidding.

If you're attending an auction for the first time, it's best to take it slow and observe the pace at which things are progressing. If need be, write down your maximum bid on a piece of paper and keep staring at it until it becomes ingrained in your memory. Do not raise your card or click the bid button just for the sake of winning the auction.

Online auctions are better in this aspect. The energy of the room will not infect you. However, seasoned bidders prefer in-person events for the thrill of it. Either way, fix your maximum bid amount and stick to it no matter what. Do not exceed it even by a single cent.

Speak Up

Too many novice bidders are timid when it comes to stating their bid. It isn't enough for you to simply hold your card up. Some auctioneers direct the bid increases by stating the bids in succession. In such scenarios, you can raise your card and leave it at that.

Most auctions will require you to speak up. Make sure you yell your number out as loud as possible. You might draw a few chuckles, but it's better to get laughed at and win a bid than to remain silent and stew in disappointment.

So yell out as loud as you possibly can and raise your hand as clearly as possible so that you draw the auctioneer's attention. You'd be surprised at how many people lose bids because they didn't speak loudly enough for the auctioneer to hear them.

Late Bids

This is a staple tactic that seasoned bidders do. They let the auction carry on initially and allow bids to keep rising. At first, there will be a number of bidders, and as prices go higher, the list whittles down to a few people. As this list shrinks in size, the confidence of the remaining bidders increases. They think they're about to win the auction.

At the last moment, as the bid is going twice, the seasoned veteran yells out a price that is $5,000 higher than the current bid. This shocks the audience as well as the bidder, who thought they were in the lead. This hesitation produces a delay and, as a result, the seasoned pro wins the auction. It saves them energy yelling out pointlessly and it also puts them in great position to win the auction.

Watch out for this tactic in the auctions you're taking part in. Always have your maximum bid in mind and know how much you have to get close to it. If someone tries to shock you in this manner, remember to bid an amount that is greater than what they just bid.

There is another psychological effect this tactic creates on the person who thought they were about to win. They mentally prepare themselves to receive the property at a certain price. Once the price is hiked at the last minute, they have to deal with not just the disappointment of having it snatched away from them, but also the fact that the same property looks more expensive.

They need to yell a counter bid within a few seconds to stay in it. Processing all of these emotions in such a small amount of time takes a lot of practice. If you find yourself in this position, try to remain as calm as you can and do not congratulate yourself until you've been declared the winner. Always assume someone else is going to come in and hike the bid on you.

Chapter 11: You've Won. What Next?

So you've won the auction and find yourself the proud owner of a property deed. Congratulations are in order! What now? There's another step you'll need to take care of before you can start monetizing your property. This has to do with the title.

In a typical real estate sale, the title you receive is called a "warranty title". This means the title is completely clean and comes without any encumbrances. It can be insured against safely and no one else has any claims on it. These titles have been vetted by title insurance companies and have passed stringent tests.

The title you receive from the county after a deed auction is not a warranty title. Instead, it's a sheriff's deed (also known as a tax deed or constable's deed.) You cannot sell this title easily to anyone else for fair market value. In order to do that, you'll have to convert it to a warranty deed.

The good news is that doing this is fairly simple. You need to hire an attorney who will file what is called a "quiet title action". This is a simple process whereby the attorney approaches the court and files a legal notice in the relevant dailies asking anyone who has any claims on your title to step forward and make themselves known.

The length of time that this notice needs to run is different. You typically don't need to worry about anyone stepping forward if the property is outside the redemption period (in the case of penalty states.) Once this process is complete, you'll have a clean title on your hands and you can put it to whatever use you'd want to.

This is why I had mentioned earlier that most buyers of tax deeds will not receive financing. The title is unclean and even the hardest of money lenders will balk at lending against such a title. There's no way they have any guarantees they can recover their money, after all.

The cost of filing a quiet title action is somewhere between $1,500 to $4,000. This isn't much of an expense when you consider the five figures or more you'll pay to acquire the deed at the auction.

Alternatives

If you happen to acquire the property for an extremely low price and wish to flip it for a quick profit, applying for a clean title doesn't make sense. You can do it, but it's likely that this process will create larger timelines. Besides, if the property needs fixing, then it doesn't make sense to do this unless you're willing to undertake repairs yourself.

In such cases, it makes sense to sell the property to a wholesaler. Real estate wholesaling is a gray area that can make a few people uncomfortable. However, there's nothing illegal about the process, and from the seller's standpoint (you're the seller) there's nothing to worry about other than having your time wasted.

Wholesalers are people who don't have the cash to purchase the property but have a buyer that does. The way it works is that the sales deed lists their name on it but gives them the option to assign the contract to their end buyer. They assign it for a higher price than what you receive, and they make a profit.

When it comes to regular property sales, wholesaling doesn't make the most sense. This is because such properties are covered by real estate agents and other investors know about them. The best wholesale leads (from the wholesaler's perspective) comes from deed auctions. These aren't as well known or covered and there are many investors in such places who are looking to flip the property for a quick profit.

Pursuing the wholesale option is sensible if you happen to be investing outside your neighborhood or state. You're not going to spend too much time rehabbing the place so you want to flip it quickly. The best way to do this is place ads in the local classifieds about "handyman specials" or contact people who post those "we buy ugly houses" signs.

You might even be contacted by people if you place a "for sale" sign in the front yard. Keep in mind that wholesaling works very well for residential properties. It's not very efficient with commercial or industrial properties since there just isn't enough secured demand for them.

Once a wholesaler contacts you, ask them for proof of funds. This is usually a letter from an investor or their bank statement that indicates they have the cash ready to be able to pay you. The wholesaler will request to take pictures of the property. Accompany them just for safety's sake. It is your property after all. Once this is done, you'll need to approach an attorney and have them draw a sales agreement. Some experienced investors choose to do this themselves but it's best to get it done professionally, especially if it's your first time doing this. You'll be selling the property through what's known as a "quit claim" deed. This deed contains no warranties. It's justified because you're selling the property at a deep discount to market prices.

The end buyer of the property is going to likely be a rehabber who will invest in the title to bring it up to scratch, along with the rest of the property. These people typically apply the 70 percent rule when offering a final price.

They subtract the cost of repairs from the ARV of the property and offer no more than 70% of this number. You will have run comps on the property before the bidding, so this should help you ballpark the amount of profit the rehabber is making along with the repairs they're budgeting. Negotiate accordingly.

Once the title is transferred and you have the money in your account, you're done with the property. Hopefully, you earned a tidy profit!

Chapter 11: Miscellaneous State Level Information

When writing a book of this kind, there's a danger of oversimplifying a lot of the processes that some states undertake. This is because it's up to the discretion of county-level officials to decide how to run their auctions and it's close to impossible to collect all of this data accurately.

Therefore, I'll stick to pointing out some of the more notable exceptions to the information that has been provided in this book. For starters, you will recall that I had mentioned that it's possible to buy tax liens OTC or over the counter. In reality, some states don't offer this option.

Alaska, for example, doesn't offer OTC sales. So make sure you check with the local county before registering for their auction. The best way to figure out their rules is to simply type in the county's name in an online search and read their terms and conditions. These documents will be filled with legal-sounding language, but don't let this put you off.

Tax Liens And Deeds Investing

If you'd rather speak to someone over the phone, then calling the county offices works well. You'll be able to speak to someone who can help you directly. Be warned that you'll be directed to their online page by default, so you'll need to sweet talk your way forward.

Alaska is also an example that is unfriendly towards individual investors. This is because all of its tax deed auctions are attended only by its municipalities. Individuals are not allowed to enter. It's an extreme example of a state going out of its way to shut everyone else out. Municipalities can resell the properties to individuals but this is a long drawn-out process. As such, it's best to stay away from the state.

In some states, the tax lien takes priority over a state lien. The relative seniority of liens is something you'll need to research on and ask officials about since this is an important factor in deciding whether to invest in a lien or not. Pay special attention to bid minimums in deed states.

For example, in Arkansas, the lien amount is not the required minimum. Instead, it's the county assessor's value that is the minimum amount required. California is an example of a deed state where the minimums are extremely low - sometimes even lower than the outstanding lien amount.

Tax Liens And Deeds Investing

Premium bidding systems pose a problem for mathematically-challenged investors. Further compounding the issue is that states vary the way in which the premium is treated. For example, Colorado keeps the premium, as well as does not pay any interest on this amount. It pays interest at a puny nine points above the federal discount rate. Given that rates are hovering near zero, one wonders why Colorado even bothers holding auctions.

Some states offer different statutory rates depending on the redemption period. Indiana is an example of this. In addition, Indiana is a premium bid lien state and both amounts receive different interest rates.

A state such as Hawaii offers different properties depending on which part of the state you're bidding in. For example, the Eastern side offers primarily agricultural lots and lots with a lot of jungle, whereas the lots auctioned through the Western office offer residential and more traditional lots that occur to people when they think of property.

Texas, similarly, offers a wide variety of lots. While the state offers the highest rates of return, you should do your homework on them since many of these lots tend to be in the middle of nowhere. Some states offer different redemption periods depending on their condition.

For example, Illinois offers a two-year redemption period of regular properties, but if there was work put into the property, this tends to turn that redemption period to three years.

The bottom line is that there are huge discrepancies between states in the way they handle things. You should always conduct thorough research before registering for an auction. Consider this book your starting point to understand the factors involved in an auction. Your next step should be to gather the details from the county offices where you plan on bidding.

Conclusion

Tax liens and deeds are an extremely lucrative way of earning a profit in real estate. It doesn't require massive specialized knowledge or anything of the sort. Most of the challenges of investing via tax liens and deeds come from the relative obscurity in which these sales take place.

Take your time to learn all of the rules and regulations in place before choosing to bid in these auctions. The rules change from time to time, and the modes of these auctions change along with them. One of the most common changes that's occurring is the migration of these auctions from in-person to online channels.

The key thing to keep in mind is that, once you acquire a property, you need to do something with it. Do not sit on the property or leave it vacant since this results in its value decreasing even more. An empty property will attract pests, squatters and other undesirable elements.

This is especially true when you win a tax deed auction. It's best to prepare beforehand and note the numbers of any wholesalers in the area. This way, the minute you win the auction, you can contact them and get the process started. Always remember to ask for proof of funds. It needs to be a letter signed by the end buyer's bank along with a bank statement that has been certified by the manager.

The worst-case scenario for you when dealing with a wholesaler is that your time will be wasted. You don't need to worry about fraud or any such criminal activity. Ensure the funds are in your account, and only then should you transfer the title.

A common question new investors ask is whether they ought to invest in liens or in deeds? The choice depends on you. The lien investing process is less strenuous in terms of the amount of money needed. The exits from the investment are clearly defined and it's a good way to earn income passively.

However, the upside is capped. While there is the potential of you lucking into winning a lien on an excellent property and then having the owner default, thereby giving you potential ownership, the odds of you actually ending up with the property is remote. Unless you have the resources to compete in a deed auction, you're going to end up owning a property that no one wants.

For this purpose, it's important that you research the

property thoroughly before you buy it. The same advice applies to deed investing as well. While deed investing requires a higher dollar amount, the returns you can earn are higher. You'll need to put in more effort into checking the property's condition and into its ability to generate the returns you want.

You'll also need to take great care when it comes to the auction process since the higher dollar amount can magnify any mistakes you make. As I mentioned in the previous chapter, this book is a starting point in your lien-investing journey. There are many counties out there and all of them have their own quirks when it comes to holding auctions.

Their terms will vary greatly and you might find that, at some of the smaller counties, the way in which these terms are offered might change depending on the type of property being auctioned. It's easy to get intimidated by these variations, so it's best for you to take your time and define things so you have a thorough understanding of what you are getting into.

Stick to these and stay away from bidding on anything that doesn't make sense to you. This way, you'll reduce your chances of making a mistake.

Follow the tips outlined in this book and I'm positive that you'll earn steady returns by investing in tax liens and deeds. Do let me know how this book helped you and what you think of the information that has been presented.

I wish you all the luck and profits in your efforts!

Bluesource And Friends

This book is brought to you by Bluesource And Friends, a happy book publishing company.

Our motto is **"Happiness Within Pages"**

We promise to deliver amazing value to readers with our books.

We also appreciate honest book reviews from our readers.

Connect with us on our Facebook page www.facebook.com/bluesourceandfriends and stay tuned to our latest book promotions and free giveaways.

Citations

Cussen, M. P. (2020, May 6). *Investing in Property Tax Liens*. Investopedia. https://www.investopedia.com/articles/investing/061313/investing-property-tax-liens.asp

Kelley, D. (2020, January 4). *Investing In Tax Liens Fraught With Risk | Bankrate.com*. Bankrate. https://www.bankrate.com/investing/investing-in-tax-liens-fraught-with-risk/

Lyons, R. (2020). *Tax Lien Investing: Double-Digit Returns – But Is This Investment Right for You?* Investorjunkie.Com. https://investorjunkie.com/real-estate/tax-lien/

Made in the USA
Las Vegas, NV
18 March 2024